GOOD MORNING
SUNSHINE!

by

Bil Keane

FAWCETT GOLD MEDAL • NEW YORK

GOOD MORNING SUNSHINE!

Published by special arrangement with The Register & Tribune
Syndicate, Inc. by Fawcett Gold Medal Books, a unit of CBS
Publications, the Consumer Publishing Division of CBS Inc.

ISBN: 0-449-14356-2

Printed in the United States of America

First Fawcett Gold Medal printing: August 1980

10   9   8   7   6   5

"You forgot to say 'Once upon a time.'"

"It's a good thing PJ was born. We're easier to divide up now, aren't we?"

"I'm goin' back to bed. I've got some sleep left in me."

"Stop that barking, Barfy! Don't you know PJ
is takin' a nap?"

"Is kittycat bionic, Mommy? She can jump real high."

"I don't WANNA grow up to be big and tall.
I'm going to be a jockey."

"This fountain doesn't have very good aim."

"Our basketball went in a puddle."

"These crayons won't go where I want them to go."

"Guess I better not wear these raggedy under-
pants in case I get in an accident."

"Barfy broke his necklace."

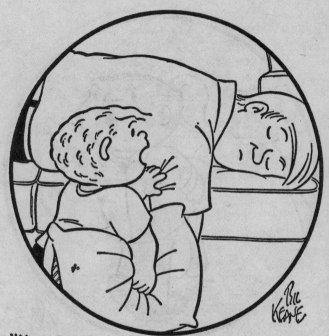

"Here, Daddy. Do you want a pillow? Daddy?
DADDY!"

"Mommy, is 'maybe' closer to 'yes' than it is to 'no?'"

"That's Adam. God made him and he grew up
to be Tarzan."

"Look how long Daddy's lap is!"

"Are kittycat's whiskers for anything or are they just decorations?"

"Billy's aiming his fist at me!"

"I'm glad I don't have to use my tongue as a wash cloth."

"I promised them."

"I hurt the knee of my finger!"

"My mother says will you tell me when it's four
o'clock 'cause that's when I hafta
go home."

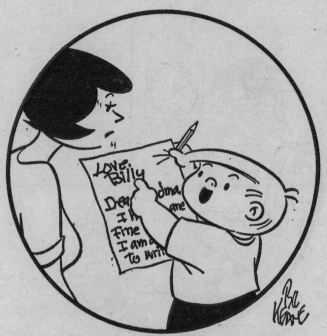

"It's so Grandma doesn't have to read the
whole letter to find out who it's from."

"Mommy says I can't come out, but wait a
minute — I'll ask my daddy."

"When will my voice get IMPORTANT like Daddy's?"

"Okay, but just a LITTLE smidgen, not a BIG smidgen."

"This is water from the bathroom. I wanted KITCHEN water."

"You know what grandma always says: 'A washed pot never boils.'"

"Crayons smell better."

"Boy! These sure are hard to unzip!"

"I've finished my bath, Mommy!"

"Six in non-smoking and as close to the lavatory as possible."

"We're gonna play in our house 'cause the
Isbell's mommy is tired and wants
to take a nap."

"Look at the pretty birds high in the sky."

"Those are bugs and they're right here."

"We're gonna speed up the sliding board."

"Is your back all right, Mommy? Billy just
stepped on a crack."

"Why CAN'T we stop to look at the O'Connors'
new kittens?"

"MARCO! . . . POLO! . . . MARCO! . . . POLO! . . ."

"Could you put it in two bags? We have
two dogs.".

"Okay! Let's watch the movie!"

"My straw has something stuck in its throat."

"Remember, Jeffy—if you win me you hafta jump over the net and tell me."

"This shirt has too many buttons."

"PJ's making ice cream SOUP!"

"Daddy watched himself to sleep."

"Do they only have one channel?"

"Mommy! We all beat Daddy! We all beat Daddy! Now he has to buy ice cream for everybody!"

"It made the childrens laugh and play 'cause lambs aren't allowed on the school bus."

"The dandelions are old now — they have gray hair."

"We ate dinner already, Grandma, but we didn't have any DESSERT yet!"

"Shall I wake Daddy up or let that fly do it?"

"Why are you sharpening your nails?"

"Mommy! Does this need first aid or just
second aid?"

"Daddy, you have an acupuncture."

"We're fixing' breakfast. Which do you like
— Sugar Whoops or Popsie
Wheat Stars?"

"Look, that lady can blow two bubbles at once."

"It's a vest. Daddy wears it when he needs more pockets."

"All these little golf clubs are called 'notes.'"

"Hereafter when we come here you're not to
wear those corduroy pants."

"I'll zip Mommy up while you're gone."

"Can I ask God to bless Daddy even though he's out of town?"

"This is a NEAT gas station! They have a
candy machine, a soda machine, a
sandwich machine . . ."

"I know our phone number. It's
1,2,3,4,5,6,7,8,9,0."

"You're not supposed to hit girls unless they're
your sister."

"Mr. Horton said I'm full of soup, but I had peanut butter for lunch!"

"Wish I could lie in a circle like Kittycat."

"Don't you have any sheets with animals or cartoons on them, Grandma?"

"Tell me a story about me."

"Who took the pencil that belongs here?"   "Not me."
"Not me."

"Who got out all   "Ida Know."
these toys?

"Will you wait a minute when the light
changes? My Mommy wants to turn!"

"Mommy, how do you spell 'at'? And go slow when you're spelling it."

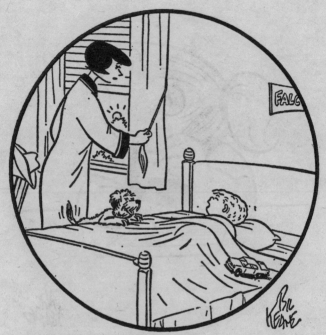

"I'm still tired. Does it have to be tomorrow
already?"

"Mommy, the baby sitter is crying."

"Foot fault, double fault, play a let!
Lob it up, talk a lot, take the set!"

"Shouldn't you go home now, Robby? We're
going to have dinner."

"That's okay. I'll just stand here and watch."

"Boy, Daddy! You sure can cook!"

"Yeeulk! I don't blame caterpillars for turning
into butterflies."

"Hi, Grandma! We had to take a bath 'cause
you were comin.' "

"Sucking those things will make you bald like Kojak."

"WALK!"

"Corn really tastes good on these rollers."

"NO...STOP-PING...EX-CEPT..."

"Daddy! Will you back up so I can finish reading that one?"

"Ants play 'Follow the Leader' a lot."

"If this is a nursery, where are all the babies?"

"I wanna play school, too!"

"I think we'll retire number 52."

"Well, off to the rat race."   "Well, off to the mouse race."

"We'll be the Republicans and you be the Democrats."

"The bus didn't show up so I said you'd drive us."

"Couldn't I wait till after eleven o'clock to talk
to God? The rates are lower then."

"We don't 'have to start bein' good till after
Thanksgiving, do we, Mommy?"

"That's not Turkey-Lurkey, is it?"

"Don't call me 'sweetheart' while the guys are here."

"I hope the police know we f'got our key and don't think we're robbers."

"What did PJ say now?"

"On Dasher, on Dancer, on Prancer and Vix-
en, on Comet, on Cupid, on Donder
and Blitzen!"

"You didn't say Rudolph."

"Is a Christmas list s'posed to be the stuff
you're gettin' or the stuff you're givin'?"

"What are the names of Santa's other elves
besides Sleepy, Dopey and Sneezy?"

"Is this picture of Santa good enough for us to
have printed on our Christmas card?"

"That's a GIRLS' room!"

"I can't reach the paper towels."

"I'll need more than that. I'm writing to Santa Claus."

"Do Santa and his mommy   "No, just elves."
have any childrens?"

"Why did Scrooge say 'Bah, Hamburg!'?"

"Remember last week when Mommy phoned
you 'cause I was bad? Well I've been
very good ever since."

"I hope Santa doesn't talk to teachers."

"Only $7.95."

"Oh, come let us adore me . . ."

"I'm not tellin' ANYBODY what I want for
Christmas 'cause I already told Santa."

"I keep tryin' real hard to close my eyes,
Mommy, but I can't get to sleep."

"Santa comes down the chimney 'cause if he came through the door it might slam and wake everybody up."

"Santa forgot some things. How many days till
my birthday?"

" . . . and a dump truck . . . and a book
about whales . . . and a football . . . and
candy in my stocking . . . and . . . "

"I was over at Eddie's house and now I know
what I want for next Christmas."

"My mom's mad 'cause daddy gave her a blender. She says she wanted one, but not for Christmas."

"Billy! It's almost midnight. Billy? You wanted
to see the new year come in, Billy? . . .
Billy? . . ."

"Happy Birthd . . . I mean, Merry Chr . . . I mean Happy New Year, Grandma!"

"She's pickin' ornaments."

"I built some lollipops!"

"Look at it with your EYES, not your hands!"

"If I catch you talking once more you're going to sit with the girls!"

"Everybody be quiet! I'm gonna catch up on some of my shuteyes!"

"Mommy, the picture's a little woozy."

Have Fun with the Family Circus

☐ ANY CHILDREN?	14116	$1.50
☐ DADDY'S LITTLE HELPERS	14384	$1.50
☐ DOLLY HIT ME BACK!	14273	$1.50
☐ GOOD MORNING SUNSHINE!	14356	$1.50
☐ FOR THIS I WENT TO COLLEGE?	14069	$1.50
☐ NOT ME!	14333	$1.50
☐ I'M TAKING A NAP	14144	$1.50
☐ LOOK WHO'S HERE	14207	$1.50
☐ PEACE, MOMMY, PEACE	14145	$1.50
☐ PEEKABOO! I LOVE YOU!	14174	$1.50
☐ WANNA BE SMILED AT?	14118	$1.50
☐ WHEN'S LATER, DADDY?	14124	$1.50
☐ MINE	14056	$1.50
☐ SMILE!	14172	$1.50
☐ JEFFY'S LOOKIN' AT ME!	14096	$1.50
☐ CAN I HAVE A COOKIE?	14155	$1.50
☐ THE FAMILY CIRCUS	14068	$1.50
☐ HELLO, GRANDMA?	14169	$1.50
☐ I NEED A HUG	14147	$1.50
☐ QUIET! MOMMY'S ASLEEP!	13930	$1.50